Meditation

Initiation series (II)

Based on channeled information by L/L Research (Kentucky)

Derivative Work by Jochen Blumenthal

© 2018 *Das Gesetz des Einen*-Verlag (Deutschland)
Jochen Blumenthal, Bessemerstr. 82, 10. OG Süd, 12103 Berlin
Email: kontakt@dasgesetzdeseinen.de

ISBN 978-3-945871-24-9

Contents

Preface

This booklet is a plea for meditation, not only for the individual but for the human society as a whole. It is to inspire, motivate und explain; thereby admittedly proposing indeed uncommon, new and provoking views, without however wanting to force something upon the reader. It addresses spiritual seekers.

These texts are derivative works – an adaptation of originally channeled messages. My gratitude therefore goes to Don Elkins, Carla L. Rueckert and her husband Jim McCarty investing their life energy into the spiritual edification of their fellow men.

In Love and Light,
Jochen Blumenthal

Bochum, July 2018

1 The knowledge of the Creator

Through your meditations you may obtain great lessons. The first and the greatest of all is that of love and what can be obtained through this love.

Through love you receive all your faith and through your faith, your desires to serve the Creator in which way that you have chosen.

When looked upon in the right manner there is no other force in your universe that can possess more teachings for your effort.

It is within this means that you are to share with the others the knowledge of the Creator and of His creation. You shall learn and come to a greater understanding of all creation.

With meditation, individually and with others, you may gain the knowledge in which you seek to serve and the knowledge of the Creator to serve.

2 All you can give

True progress occurs beyond the dimensions of time and space.

What you do for one person you'll do for all.

Your meditation is the entirety of all that you can give.

Continue to pursue your seeking and keep yourself, through daily meditation, well-grounded in the Creation of the Father, for there is a lot of work to do.

3 From meditation to service

The importance of meditation cannot be over-emphasized. Through this technique you will receive answers to all of your questions.

It may be difficult to realize this, but it is true. All of your questions can be reduced to an extremely simple concept which you can become aware of in meditation.

Once you have achieved this you will be ready to serve, just as others have served and are now serving upon your planet. Follow their example and spend time in meditation.

Qualify yourself to reach out your hand to your fellow man and lead him out of the darkness of confusion back into the light that he seeks.

4 The simple thought of absolute love

We have lost our awareness of the Creator's plan to provide for His children, to provide for their very desire and to provide a state of perfection. We humans have lost the awareness that is rightfully ours. And why have we lost it? Because we have focused our attention upon our own devices and inventions. Thus we let ourselves become hypnotized by our own playthings and our ideas. In his mind, man is still a child.

All this can easily be remedied, and man can again come back to an appreciation of reality rather than appreciating the illusion which he created in his mind. All that is necessary for this, is that man avails himself to this appreciation of reality in meditation. For by this he stills his active conscious mind which is continually seeking stimulus within this very false illusion which has developed over so many centuries upon this planet. In this way very rapidly he can return to an appreciation of the reality in the functioning of the real creation.

That is the only reality that surrounds the reality of the love generated by his creation which in turn generated himself and all of the beings and all of the animal life and all of the bird life and all of the fishes in the sea and all of the vegetation, all of the planets, all of the stars, and all of the systems that surround us.

Our illusion is very complex but it is meaningless. Our cities, our political systems, our concept of science and of philosophy, they are all complex. They require great intellectual ability to encompass them, and yet they are nothing compared to the one simple Thought of our Creator who created us and the real creation: the simple Thought of absolute love.

This is whereto man on Earth must return if he wants to know reality: this simple Thought of absolute love, a Thought of total unity with all his brothers and sisters regardless of how they might express themselves or whom they might be, for this is the original Thought of the Creator.

Our creation supports us. It was designed in thought by our Creator to support and to provide us with all of your desires. It was the Thought of our Creator that each part of this creation should serve all other parts, for this is the Thought of absolute love, the Thought of total service. When man on Earth is once more able to realize this Thought and express it in every aspect, then will he know his creation, for then he will be at one with this Thought and this love.

Seek this understanding in meditation, for all rewards are in you. Return to the simplicity that is the creation. Still the conscious mind and become aware of what love is.

5 Transformation

Meditation is of utmost importance.

Meditation will allow you to become totally aware of the concepts of the true creation. These concepts are very simple, but they cannot be communicated with words alone.

When you become aware of these concepts in their entirety, your thinking will be transformed – in a transformation that you desire. If you did not desire it you would not be seeking it.

This transformation is necessary if you are to be totally effective in serving the Creator.

6 Feed your faith and your understanding

Wisdom is a rather lonely matter. One who places the burden of wisdom on him or herself should be ready to accept this truth.

That which you know you are to be careful of, for what you know in the real creation has power. And that which you desire is all of the direction which that power will be aimed at.

But have faith in what you know and what you are learning. Feed your faith and your understanding through meditation.

The farther that you go along this path the more meaningful you will find this simple statement: meditate.

It begins as a simple process and little by little it becomes the way in which you live. Observe it as you progress along your own spiritual path.

7 The intellectual knowledge of faith

Various methods are of aid to you in progressing on your spiritual path and serving your fellow men and Earth. I suggest to you to use one of them mostly for it will be most beneficial to you: your meditation.

In your periods of meditation you shall attain knowledge – independently from the intellectual mind. When you face situations in your daily life this knowledge shall penetrate from within you and shall function through you.

This knowledge and this growth will give you the faith which is doing you so good. Liberate that faith which is contained within your intellect. The intellectual faith is also quite valuable and is also a need to your meditation. The growth of this intellectual faith comes about by your understanding.

Each difficulty or each situation which you experience contains truth. But within this illusion the truth of each situation is very difficult to find by utilizing your thoughts. Allow the intellect to be guided by meditation and it shall be able to find the great lessons which your life has on offer for you.

In many circumstances the situation will try greatly your confidence in the world of your Creator. You shall experience times when you shall question His existence. This is normal in your growth for your intellect does continue to operate. This is the path of the human intellect.

Yet, each time you question, turn to your meditation.

Meditate upon this question and the awareness and the answer which is needed shall come to you.

In this way the intellect is aided, for seeing the truth and finding the answers in meditation gives you the intellectual knowledge of faith. You may accept the inner guidance and many situations will present themselves for that.

Do not allow your intellect to be the only means of prayer. Seek the inner guidance in all situations through meditation.

8 The fetters of our own measurement systems

How would you describe what you do in your meditation? How do you measure your success? How do you grade yourself?

Unfortunately, it is an inevitable habit of the human beings upon this planet to want to develop a type of grading system, even for those things for which they don't have a grading system available.

That which is measured is inevitably lost. What you measure is that what has been expended. In meditation nothing is expended. Meditation is a becoming. A becoming aware of that which already is in a timeless fashion. One cannot grade it for it is entirely a living activity. Not living in the sense of this illusion but living because eternity lives. It is beyond that which you may know as judging.

To the human mind that which it perceives about itself as progress can be compared to a great coral reef. He observes that which has been left behind by previous efforts, even if this is nothing more than a pile of used physical vehicles. He can see them, he can measure them and is satisfied with this.

Meditation however follows exactly the opposite way.

Free yourself from the desire to measure your progress in meditation. Free yourself from the fetters of human systems of measurement for that which you really desire is measureless and limitless.

Simply allow yourself to seek and to accept through meditation the contact with our Creator. This is your task as a portion of the creation.

9 Adjusting the schedule to your meditation

Even though the benefit of meditation is with you and needs no measurement, will you need to honor your daily habits and necessities so that you can find time for meditation.

But do not allow your daily activities to encroach upon your mediation any more than absolutely necessary.

Sometimes you have to temporarily pause your meditation because you have so many things to do. It is your decision. Try to order your daily life in such a way that you have time for meditation.

Each day as you continue to meditate it will seem to become easier to adjust your meditation to your schedule. This is due to the fact that your sense of values is shifting and the realization winning through that all problems and questions will be solved and answered through meditation.

Do not hold any recriminations toward yourself if you are unable to adhere to your meditation. Simply come back when you are ready for it. Even if it appears as if regular meditation meant forming a habit, it is not really so because a habit doesn't automatically give benefit.

10 What is not demonstrated is not understood

A high energy level in your meditation does not automatically indicate that you have learned the messages that you hear. It only indicates a desire to meditate and to learn. Other desires can intervene.

To understand the messages that you hear in a meditation with an unusually high energy level you ought to let it leak over afterwards into your everyday thinking. If you do this you will find your way how to demonstrate what you have learned.

At this point true understanding begins, for that which is not demonstrated is not understood. This is not to say that a high level of energy during your meditation is not valuable. It is very valuable, but this energy must, like any other power, be guided carefully or its power can be dissipated or wrongly used.

11 The frog

Consider a simple frog.

Suddenly he is thrust into the wet wonderland which from now on is his home. He is almost still transparent when he moves with many others of his kind and evades many enemies.

Gradually he attains shape and color. He discovers that he can make sounds and that he can take life and give life. He discovers that his consciousness is daily flooded with many thousands of images and that he has great power in his hands. And that he has a destiny which he must follow.

One day the frog is no more, for its body is no longer inhabited and sinks back into the bottom of the pond from where it originated.

This frog is a very important person to himself. His awareness is very central and that which he loves and that which he dislikes are very real to him.

We humans are aware that a frog is a frog. Now, who is right?

The frog is correct, we are correct, and both of us are we yet incorrect, for the nature of both is consciousness – consciousness that comes from one source and which is going ultimately back to its own source.

There is no beginning and no end. There is only the unity, the freedom of choice and the joy of reunion.

There is always much you may do to be of service. There are always lessons to learn. There is a reality to this illusion, but remember the frog:

You are a prince to yourself and your right and your wrong are extremely important to you, and that which you love and that which you dislike is very real to you.

Allow your consciousness to rise into the light which created you. All questions will be answered for you will know then where you are and who you are, and that all is well.

12 The acquisition of understanding

The acquisition of understanding is not the phenomenon which you probably think it is. The acquisition of understanding is part of something much more basic. It does not come before this basic quality but rather is a result of this basic quality: One can only acquire understanding to that level which one's own desire for understanding has reached.

Desire, my friend, is probably also not what you think it is. Desire is a great deal more than you think.

The desire of a human being is the human being.

It is its directional movement. This motion is the expression of one's basic consciousness and is the most basic thing about one.

What one desires, and the purity of that desire, becomes and is the individual once it is aware that this is true.

The being that is centered within its desire becomes whole and unified.

This life, my friend, is a whole, it is one thing: an interconnected galaxy of time, space and meaning. Nothing may be untwined from anything else, for all is one.

There is no strain or confusion for a human being who realized this for he is aware at all time of who he is: He is the one who desires that which he desires. He is a seeker of truth. He is on a path. That which the path offers to him is what he is looking at, is what he is learning, and is what he is demonstrating.

If he discovers that he has not followed all of his steps he learns from this discovery and never leaves the pattern of his desire.

13 Knitting patterns

You may compare the self-aware existence with a knitted garment. Each stitch is connected with another stitch. As it comes off the needles it is held safely in place.

The attempt to analyze one's life by means of external and intellectual concepts is much like removing one's stitches from the needles. It is very easy for them to get misplaced or temporarily lost and it may take some time for these stitches to be properly discovered again and put back into pattern.

Therefore, it is much better to do without this intellectual picking. It is much better to simply accept one's existence and realize at all times who one is and what one is seeking.

If one can do this it matters not whether one is sick or well or whether one is rich or poor for these things are minor details having little to do with the purpose for which your life has been dedicated.

14 The demonstration of the sweets-yogi

The journey of seeking leads you to each item of information which you obtain. If your seeking is not ready to absorb this information then you will not demonstrate this information and you will therefore not have this information. It will not be your information.

There once was a yogi. To him came a mother with her child. She asked the wise man: "Please tell him to stop eating sweets (all the time)." "You're welcome," said the yogi, "but please come back in seven days."

When the mother came back seven days later, the yogi told the child that it should stop eating sweets. The mother thanked him and wanted to leave. But then she turned around and asked: "And why couldn't you say this to my child already a week earlier?"

"Because I first need to stop eating sweets myself." replied the yogi.[1]

That which is not seen through you is not within you.

There is indeed the possibility of something like a cosmic indigestion. However, this is not the fault of the information or the fault of the entity who is not completely ready to demonstrate this information. It is simply a slight mismatching of information and it makes no difference to the seeking.

The true difficulty is due to the intellectual efforts to analyze

---

[1] This short story is an addition of the author.

and to predict items which are beyond the intellect.

There are many things which one may think and man is a creator. Man creates many, many thoughts and lives with these thoughts. These thoughts are his thoughts. He does not create them to fly away. He creates them to surround him and they surround him more and more as he thinks upon the same thoughts.

If you wish to have a certain thought about you, then think it, my friend.

If the thought which you are entertaining is not full of faith, hope, charity, love and concern for the spiritual welfare of your fellow man then you may put this thought aside and you will not be responsible for its generation.

15 In the next dimension

If you could be in the next higher dimension you would see your thoughts. You would see your emotions.

You would discover for yourself how very undesirable it is to surround yourself with those things which cause fear, sickness, pain and lack.

You would see the great strides that can be made by the constant generation of thoughts of the Creator.

The intellect cannot understand these matters and for this reason it can only be recommended to regularly meditate so that you become more conscious of the Creator's thoughts. Words can only approximately describe what is conveyed to you in meditation.

Concentrate upon your desires, upon your inner desire. Do not be afraid of any information but only know who you are and what you desire.

Love and our light, great beauty, galaxies of bursting stars, unlimited thoughts and dreams and great ecstasy – all of these things are in the creations of the Father and they are yours.

Lift up your heart, for there is much to rejoice concerning.

16 The door

What can the spiritual worlds give us?

Most of all a door. Only a doorway. Only a suggestion: the suggestion of another world, of another complete reality.

A reality that transcends this reality, that includes this reality, that explains this reality, that will completely outlast this reality and to which you will return after this brief experience upon the earth plane.

It is the suggestion of eternity. And a suggestion as to how to approach this doorway – through meditation.

Meditation is the most efficient way of approaching this door and developing the desire within you to go through this door. That alone will lead you through. Meditation makes it possible to approach this door.

17 Seed of meditation

What do you seek?

You are already aware of the very seed of that which you seek.

What are you going to do to find it?

Look at your meditation as the seed which is growing in the rich soil of your physical existence. It will bear fruit within your existence.

And the fragrance and the beauty which meditation sheds throughout the illusion will last far beyond the illusory flower, for the gifts of this fruit last forever.

Allow the seed of meditation to be endlessly nurtured within each day.

That which you need to do to bloom will come to you. The fruit which you need to supply to be of service to others will be possible for you to produce. The energy which you need to grow and flourish will be yours. And when you need rest there will be time for rest.

For once you are committed to the gentle cycles of eternity the physical illusion very quietly falls into place.

18 The service of the blade of grass and the service of the tree

Some people are already aware of their need to serve their fellow man. This awareness is a very natural thing. It is a product of maintained contact with reality.

Many people are not aware of the need for service although the Creation is specifically designed for it. It is designed so that each provides service, freely given service, to support the rest of the Creation.

It is only necessary to look about you to realize this, to realize that all parts are performing a service.

Even though your service may seem to be extremely small, it is, I can assure you, as great as the largest service that you can think of. For service is service, regardless of how you interpret it.

A blade of grass performs a service. It performs its service to the very limit of its ability. And yet its service is a great as the service of a tree which is many times, many, many times the size the tiny blade of grass. For the tree is also performing to the limit of its ability its service.

All that is necessary is for you to recognize that this is what is occurring in the Creation that surrounds you.

All that is necessary is for you to recognize how to perform the service that you may give.

All that is necessary for you to realize this is for you to become aware of it - as simply as the blade of grass or as the tree have become aware of their service: through meditation.

For through this process you will understand and you will serve, for this you have always intended to do just as every other part of the creation of the Father.

But when man forgets the purpose of the real creation he becomes isolated, lost and unable to avail himself of the love that is given to him by the Creation.

Become aware of your service. Become aware of your purpose. Go the way of meditation and you will awaken.

You will awaken to the ecstasy that was meant to be experienced by each part of this infinite creation.

19 Negativity hinders your service

Many attempts to realize something fail due to the attention being directed onto errors and the successes to a high degree ignored. This is nothing other than negative thinking.

Actively employ the positive. Squeeze out as much as possible the negative in your thinking and also in your spiritual seeking, and your spiritual consciousness.

Meditation may relinquish, it is the answer to this problem. Meditation may answer you in subtle ways.

Concentrate your energy on the positive forces within your thinking in order that as you attempt to perform your service to the Creator, you may perform a true service and avoid limiting that service by negativity.

Remember that service to others is service to yourself. Service to others is not like service to yourself – they are identical.

There is no similarity between you and others. There is only identity. There is only completion and unity.

Therefore, that which is felt of a negative nature towards a sheep of the flock is felt towards oneself, and is felt towards the Creator. This enters the service which you are attempting to give to yourself and to the Creator through service to another and this dims the service you want to give to others.

Each person is a completely free entity whose independence must in no way be shaken and yet whose identity remains one with you.

For the human mind it is almost impossible to believe other human beings are identical to oneself while entrapped in the chemical illusion. But it is far more possible through faith that you may begin to understand that each human being whom you wish to serve is the Creator.

In a higher source, you can merge with them and allow this seed in your meditation to continue to grow.

References

Text	is based upon a message of
1	Hatonn on June 2, 1974
2	unknown
3	Hatonn on June 1, 1974
4	Hatonn on June 8, 1974
5	Hatonn on June 9, 1974
6	Hatonn on June 2, 1974
7	Hatonn on June 12, 1974
8-9	Hatonn on June 21, 1974
10-15	Hatonn on June 13, 1974
16-17	Hatonn on June 23, 1974
18-19	Hatonn on June 23, 1974

Index

About the author

Jochen Blumenthal, born 1976 near the Lake of Constance, is the German translator of the Ra Contact. In 2014 he started up the Das Gesetz des Einen-Verlag (Deutschland) publishing house to provide more of L/L Research's material in German and other languages.

Jochen has studied and worked in several fields including anthropology, political sciences, business administration and spirituality. Concluding that L/L Research's channeled information is among the most important for humanity he devotes himself to translating and publishing this information further.

Additional information

The "Das Gesetz des Einen-Verlag (Deutschland)" publishing house offers a small range of own derivative English publications since L/L Research provides all of their channeled information, and a growing number of great books, to English speaking readers.

All of L/L Research's resources are freely available online and can be purchased at the L/L online store.

Among the works of L/L Research are

- The Ra-Contact: Teaching the Law of One
- Living the Law of One, 101: The Choice
- A Wanderer's Handbook
- Channelings from the Holy Spirit
- Secrets of the UFO
- Tilting at Windmills

L/L Research's internet address is www.llresearch,org.

The "Das Gesetz des Einen-Verlag (Germany)" satellite

The "Das Gesetz des Einen-Verlag (Deutschland)" offers a growing number of translations and derivative and explanatory works based on L/L Research material. In cooperation with the Belgian translator Micheline Deschreider, and under the name "Maison d'édition La Loi

Une (Allemagne)", it also offers French versions of L/L Research's and own derivative works.

Among the publications are:

In German:

- Der Ra-Kontakt: Das Gesetz des Einen lehren
- 25 Prinzipien der Realität
- Meditation
- Lehrmeister Jesus
- Dienst der Liebe
- Bündnisbotschaften Sammelband
- Essenz I
- Außerirdische Kommunikation
- Das Gesetz des Einen leben, Das 1x1: Die Wahl (Teil I)

In French:

- Le contact Ra: La Loi Une enseignée (Trad. Micheline. Deschreider)
- Comment vivre la Loi Une, Niveau I: Le Choix (Trad. M. Deschreider)
- Vade mecum du pèlerin errant (Trad. M. Deschreider)
- 25 principes de réalité
- Méditation
- Jésus, Le Maître Enseignant (Trad. Nicolas Turban)
- Le Service d'Amour (Trad. N. Turban)

In Swedish & Dutch

- Kosmiska principer: 25 principer om verkligheten (Translation by Klas Häger)

- 25 Principer van de realiteit (Translation Coen Weesjes)

In the web

www.joth.dasgesetzdeseinen.de

www.dasgesetzdeseinen.de

www.diebrueckenrede.wordpress.com

www.laloiune.eu

L/L Research

All messages received by Carla Rueckert along with Jim McCarty, Don Elkins and many others, and all of L/L Research's works are available at

www.llresearch.org

www.ingramcontent.com/pod-product-compliance
Lightning Source LLC
Chambersburg PA
CBHW060543030426
42337CB00021B/4411

www.ingramcontent.com/pod-product-compliance
Lightning Source LLC
Chambersburg PA
CBHW060542030426
42337CB00021B/4389